Original title:
The House at Dawn

Copyright © 2025 Creative Arts Management OÜ
All rights reserved.

Author: Vivienne Beaumont
ISBN HARDBACK: 978-1-80587-152-1
ISBN PAPERBACK: 978-1-80587-622-9

Eager Hearts at the Break of Day

As sunlight peeks through sleepy blinds,
A cat's in a tangle, of the yarn it finds.
Coffee brews, a fragrant delight,
While socks vanish, to our morning fright.

Laughter bubbles, the toast is burnt,
With every sip, a new lesson learned.
The dog barks at shadows, a leaping foe,
While the clock ticks on, so slow you know.

The World Slowly Stirring Back to Life

Birds chirp with eagerness, having their say,
While squirrels dance, plotting their play.
The mailman delivers with a wink and a grin,
As the plants stretch out, eager to begin.

Neighbors stumble out in disarray,
With mismatched shoes on this sunny day.
Laughter erupts as the blender roars,
Mixing breakfast chaos, who could want more?

Traces of Night in Morning's Glow

Moonbeams linger on a sleeping face,
Pajamas still on, it's a sleepy race.
The cereal bowl sings as milk pours in,
While someone wonders where did the spoon begin?

Dreams mix with coffee, a glorious sight,
One eye still closed, the other bright.
The dog has stolen a slice of toast,
And we just laugh, it's what we love most.

Beauty Found in First Breaths

The scent of pancakes fills the air,
A talented chef—oh, what a rare affair!
The alarm clock rebels, it rings too loud,
And we wake up laughing, a sleepy crowd.

Jammies still on, a dance in the hall,
We trip over toys, it's a hilarious fall.
Morning's embrace, with its joyful cheer,
In this circus of life, we hold dear!

Harbingers of Morning

The rooster crows, a silly sound,
As cats plot mischief all around.
Coffee brews with a funny hiss,
Awake, my world, with morning bliss.

Socks unmatched, what a sight to see,
The dog's got toothpaste on its knee.
Breakfast burned, oh what a shame,
But laughter always wins the game.

Light Through the Open Window

Sunlight dances on my floor,
While guarded shadows search for more.
A squirrel steals my sandwich left,
Such audacity, where's the heft?

Birds chirp songs, a comical tune,
Outsmarted by a sneaky raccoon.
A curtain flutters, the cat is trapped,
In this morning play, all have lapped.

The First Breath of Day

The kettle whistles, a shrill alarm,
A toast pops up with a little charm.
The toasty bread does a happy flip,
While I just hope it's not a trip.

Tea leaves dance with a cheeky spin,
As morning giggles pull me in.
I trip on shoes, all in a mess,
But laughter finds me, I confess.

Dance of the Waking Hours

In this ballet of yawns and blinks,
The calendar spills all its inks.
At breakfast, cereal does a dive,
Creating chaos, it's how we thrive!

With slippers flapping, I prance about,
Too many socks, but that's no doubt.
In morning's charm, fun does abound,
With every laugh, joy is found.

New Horizons Beneath the Rising Sun

A rooster crows with a silly song,
The cat yawns wide, it won't be long.
The coffee brews with a playful hiss,
While toast pops up, a breakfast bliss.

Birds in pajamas fly by the window,
Chasing shadows, all in a row.
The sun laughs bright, spills milk on trees,
And ducks waddle by, wearing tiny fees.

Cracks of Light in the Sleeping World

The curtains twitch, a sneaky peek,
A cherry pie dreams, but it's not sleek.
The bedbugs dance, a jig in the sheets,
While socks unite in odd little fleets.

The clock strikes three, but who's keeping time?
An old cat sings a made-up rhyme.
The biscuits joke about a biscuit fight,
As grasshoppers hop, all ready for flight.

A Soliloquy of Fresh Beginnings

An onion's layers start to argue,
While spices plot in the kitchen's curfew.
Eggs roll in cases, their shell a throne,
Dreaming of omelets, all on their own.

Butter melts down, with a mischievous grin,
While pancakes flip in a swirling spin.
The syrup smiles, sweet on the side,
As breakfast becomes the whole family's pride.

Silence in the Wake of Dawn

The snoring stops as dreams hit the floor,
The dog finds sense, but can't find the door.
Socks debate on which foot to wear,
As toast gets tangled in a sticky affair.

The kettle whistles a high-pitched cheer,
While kids choose chairs with a giggly sneer.
Coffee's a wizard, casting spells on the bland,
Breakfast brigade rallies in a feast so grand.

Haikus in the Quietude

Morning sun awakes,
Socks on the wrong foot,
Coffee spills like art,
Cereal dances near.

A cat jumps in fright,
Chasing shadows of bliss,
Bagels in a race,
Toaster lost in heat.

Birds tweet absurd tunes,
While squirrels plot their schemes,
Tickling the old tree,
Nature's wildest dreams.

The clock's lost its beat,
Breakfast is a mess,
Laughter fills the space,
In this morning jest.

The Dawn Chorus

Birds chime like a band,
Worms fret beneath the ground,
A rooster starts to yell,
Echoes all around.

Coffee pot's in tug,
With spoons that runaway,
Mugs engaging in war,
As milk makes its play.

The dog steals my toast,
As I trip on a shoe,
Socks thrown in their brawl,
Who knew morning's queue?

Laughter fills the air,
As we tumble and spin,
The day is young and bright,
Let the circus begin!

Beneath the Veil of Mist

Misty morn arrives,
Fog blankets the lawn,
Marshmallows on toast,
Full moon starts to yawn.

A squirrel wears my hat,
While I search for socks,
A dance of the clumsy,
As I trip o'er rocks.

Tea kettle's a star,
Making music so sweet,
It whistles a tune,
To which we move our feet.

In the chaos of dawn,
Each giggle echoes loud,
We spark a new day,
Bold, silly, and proud.

First Light Reverie

Sunlight peeks at me,
Through curtains with flair,
A sock puppet show,
With my teddy bear.

Waffles jump and flip,
Syrup starts to race,
A butter slide's fun,
Pancakes join the chase.

Cats lounge on the rug,
While dogs play charades,
A turtleneck gets lost,
In morning escapades.

The day's just begun,
With laughter galore,
Each moment's a treat,
Let's dance on the floor!

Where Silence Meets Daylight

In the morning light, the cat yawns wide,
As the sleepy goldfish goes for a ride.
Birds tweet gossip, like it's all a show,
While shadows dance slow, on the wall they glow.

A squirrel drops acorns, what a loud thud!
It seems breakfast is now just a last-minute dud.
The mailbox swings open, a letter falls flat,
Now the day starts, with a giggle and chat.

Elysium in Morning's Embrace

Coffee percolates, a bubbling song,
The toaster pops up, and toasts go along.
A pancake flips high, what a clumsy arc!
It lands on the dog, who now sports a spark!

The shower's a symphony, soap suds parade,
Rubber ducks dance while the shampoo's delayed.
A towel on the floor is a slip and a slide,
Welcome to mornings, let the joy be the guide!

Lingering Mists and Soft Horizons

Fog rolls like laughter, in ribbons it sways,
A jogger trips over, what a funny gaze!
The sun peeks through, like a shy little child,
With shades and a hat, oh isn't it wild?

A quick game of tag with the clouds in the sky,
As daffodils gossip, by passersby.
The breeze carries whispers of yesterday's fun,
While pigeons coo secrets, the day's just begun!

Signs of Life Beneath the Veil

Under the porch lies a mystery deep,
A raccoon named Fred, who just can't keep.
Stealing the trash, with a grin ear to ear,
His antics bring laughter, what a show here!

The garden awakens, sunflowers laugh bright,
While a snail's on a quest, it's a slow-motion sight.
A ladybug twirls, on a leaf she'll reside,
In this funny little world, where peace cannot hide.

Rustling Leaves at Daybreak

Leaves whisper secrets, oh so sly,
Squirrels plotting mischief on high.
The sun peeks in, a cheeky grin,
While birdies squawk, let the fun begin!

A cat yawns wide, stretches like a star,
Chasing shadows, thinking it's bizarre.
The garden wakes, with laughter in bloom,
As bees buzz loud, dispelling the gloom.

With sleepy eyes, the windows creak,
A toast to toast, it's breakfast we seek.
The kettle whistles a morning tune,
While slippers dance 'neath the light of the moon!

Oh, the day has started, what a delight,
With all its quirks, everything feels right.
As clouds float by without a care,
Daybreak's here, and it's time to share!

The Hues of Awakening

Colors splash, like kids in a mud,
Pink and orange, just like a thud!
The sky chuckles, paints a wide grin,
As rooster crows, let the fun begin!

Coffee brews with a heart-shaped steam,
While toast pops up like a morning dream.
Butter slips and slides like it's in a race,
Breakfast is served at a wild pace!

The lamp shades dance, all jumbled and bright,
Chasing the shadows that creep from the night.
Bug zippers zoom with a dazzling hum,
A parade of laughter, here they come!

Wait for cat, oh where can she be?
Tangled in yarn or sipping her tea?
Morning's quite mad, with a skip and a hop,
In the hues of awakening, let's never stop!

When Night Meets the Light

As night slips out, morning takes a bow,
The fridge hums a tune, to wake up the cow.
With pajamas flapping all over the floor,
The day beckons, who could ask for more?

A burst of giggles fills the air,
A dog barks back, challenging the faire.
The toast takes a leap, and jam jumps too,
Mornings are wacky, with a view askew!

Sunbeams tumble through the window wide,
Chasing dust bunnies in a playful glide.
Cats stretch and yawn, dreaming of their prize,
As the clock announces its morning rise!

Time to get moving, but we trip and twirl,
Coffee spills, oh it makes us swirl!
When night meets the light, let's create a scene,
With silly moments, fit for a queen!

Echoes of a New Beginning

Waking up chirpy, a tune in my head,
With chaotic dreams that danced in my bed.
Pajamas askew and hair in a knot,
We're rolling with laughter, let's write what we jot!

The teapot whistles a high-pitched cheer,
While the cat sneaks in, giving me a leer.
The sunlight joins in on the playful spree,
Casting shadows that giggle around me!

A toast that jumps in the air just right,
Landing with butter, what a silly sight!
As the family gathers, oh what a crowd,
Echoes of joy, both silly and loud!

Morning will never be boring or plain,
With chuckles and jests that scatter like rain.
In this funny dance, life's new and bright,
Let's revel together in the morning light!

Silhouettes Against the Light

In the morning's gentle glare,
Shadows dance without a care.
Cats and dogs take their delight,
Making mischief, what a sight!

The toaster pops, a sudden cheer,
Spilling crumbs, a breakfast frontier.
Coffee steam takes playful flight,
As we chuckle at the height.

Neighbors wander, waving high,
In mismatched socks, they pass us by.
Laughter echoes, bright and clear,
As we toast to another year.

In the spectacle of morning's show,
We find the joy in ebb and flow.
With every giggle, every bite,
Our hearts feel lighter, what a height!

Familiar Footsteps in the Quietude

In the stillness, a footstep slips,
Sounding like a sitcom's quips.
Pajamas worn, one inside out,
Who said mornings can't be a hoot about?

The creaky floor sings a tune,
As the dog howls at the moon.
Sneakers squeak, a silly race,
Fleeting laughter fills the space.

With cereal thrown, a dance takes flight,
Milk spills over, oh what a plight!
Yet here we are, in this blissful mess,
Finding humor, I must confess.

Familiar footsteps, but oh what flair,
In our haven, the world's laid bare.
So we chuckle and tease with love,
As the day beams down from above!

Conversing with the Morning Breeze

The breeze arrives with a cheeky wink,
Whispering secrets - what do you think?
It tickles the curtains, it shakes the trees,
   Pulling laughter from dreaming bees.

Window pots sway, they giggle too,
Flirting with raindrops, in skies so blue.
"A dance?" says the pansy, "I'm in!"
While the daisy grins, "Let's begin!"

Over the rooftops, the chatter flies,
With every stretch, a bright surprise.
It's a banter that dries up the gloom,
Providing warmth, like a cozy room.

The morning breeze, a witty tease,
Filling hearts with hopes like these.
With every gust, a promise rings,
In its whispers, joy springs!

The Promise of a Fresh Canvas

Brush in hand, a splash of flair,
Colors collide with joy in the air.
With every stroke, I laugh and sigh,
As I paint the clouds and the sky.

A smudge of blue, now a big surprise,
Turns into a grin - how time flies!
Splatters of yellow, bright as can be,
Creating a scene, quite wild and free.

The canvas speaks in shades so bold,
Whispers of stories waiting to be told.
With hiccups of joy in every line,
Art is fun, and oh so divine!

So here's to the day, let colors clash,
In our home, we find a laugh.
Every sunrise brings a fresh start,
A blank canvas for the heart!

Dawn's Silent Lament.

Morning yawns, the sun appears,
A cat falls down, full of sneers.
Toast burns bright, the coffee's weak,
Birds chirp loud, their song unique.

A sock escapes, the door's ajar,
Chasing it, I travel far.
Pajamas tangled, hair a mess,
Who knew dawn could cause such stress?

The fridge hums softly in its spot,
While I search for what I've forgot.
Eggs in hand, I drop a few,
At least the floor enjoyed the stew.

Sunrise giggles at my plight,
As I dance around in awkward light.
Yet here I stand, silliness grown,
In dawn's embrace, I'm not alone.

Whispers of Morning Light

With sleepy eyes, I greet the day,
The toaster sparks, in disarray.
A squirrel on the window ledge,
Watches me as I lose my edge.

The kettle sings a tune so sweet,
I trip on shoes near my feet.
The fluffy dog, a couch potato,
Dreams of chasing things much greater.

Sunbeams drape like silly hats,
As I dodge wandering spats of cats.
In the kitchen, chaos reigns,
As jugs of juice spill on the plains.

The clock laughs at my morning sprint,
A dance routine, without a hint.
Though mismatched socks are all I wear,
Laughter echoes, filling the air.

Awakenings in the Quiet Hour

Waking up with sleepy sighs,
Dancing shadows meet my eyes.
A cereal box claims a prize,
As rogue milk begins to rise.

The dog wags his tail in glee,
As I bend down, knee to knee.
A stuffed frog leaps from the floor,
And lands with a splat, oh what a chore!

Bright moments spark like fireflies,
While I spill tea, oh such lies!
The chair welcomes me with a creak,
As I settle down for just a peek.

Yet outside, the sun starts its race,
With chirpy friends in a wild chase.
I sip my drink, declare a truce,
For dawn brings fun, no excuse!

Shadows Kiss the First Rays

As shadows dance on the wall,
I step out, trip, and make a call.
The broom greets me with open bristles,
While my old slippers play the whistles.

A garden gnome gives me a scare,
As dew drops fall, causing despair.
I witness ants form a parade,
While I ponder the breakfast I made.

The mailman slips, lets out a yelp,
As I munch on my veggie kelp.
Whimsical moments in dawn's embrace,
Oh how I love this charming place!

But soon the laughter fades away,
As chores beckon me to stay.
Yet in the laughter, joy unfolds,
With dawn's warmth, life never grows old.

The Pulse of a New Day

Morning light creeps in with a grin,
Cats stretch and yawn, let the chaos begin.
Coffee brews with a sizzle and pop,
Who knew waking up could be such a hop?

Toasters dance like they're on a stage,
Burnt toast jokes—oh, what a rage!
Slippers glide to the rhythm of feet,
In this symphony, can we keep the beat?

Sunshine teases with a playful wink,
As all the sleepyheads begin to think.
Mismatched socks in a daring display,
Fashion, they say, is just playfully gray!

Rise and shine, it's a brand new spree,
With laughter ringing like a bumblebee.
A pulse so lively, a beat so gay,
Who knew mornings could dance this way?

Bonfire of Old Dreams as the Sun Warms

Old dreams flicker like marshmallows bright,
Roasting on the fire, oh what a sight!
They crackle and pop, some turn to goo,
While others are burnt, say bon voyage too!

A chorus of giggles, it's quite the show,
As memories swirl, like smoke in the flow.
S'mores made of laughter and inside jokes,
Around the flames, we share silly pokes!

Sunshine spills in, warming our cheeks,
While nostalgia dances and gently squeaks.
A bonfire that fizzes, with moments passed,
As we toss our dreams in, making it last!

Good riddance to worries, let them go free,
As we bask in the glow, just you and me.
With a wink to the past, we embrace the warm,
Building new dreams in this playful form!

Dawn's Embrace for Wandering Spirits

Wandering spirits stretch with a smile,
Dancing in sunlight, it's been a while.
Tickling the flowers, whispering low,
They laugh at the shadows, putting on a show!

In the meadow where giggles collide,
Who knew butterflies had such fun inside?
Chasing the breeze and twirling in grace,
A parade of mischief in this open space!

With a wink from the dew, the day is our friend,
As the clock strikes laughter, we just can't pretend.
Hopping from clouds, sprightly and light,
The spirits embrace this radiant sight!

So come join the frolic, let your heart free,
In the dawn's embrace, just you and me.
Wandering spirits, we'll dance and we'll sing,
In the laughter of morn, life is our fling!

The Awakening of Forgotten Corners

In corners forgotten, where dust bunnies play,
A laugh in the cupboard is here to stay.
Cobwebs are giggling, shaking in cheer,
As memories stir from their slumbering sphere!

The old rocking chair moans a tune,
As sunlight pours in like a giant balloon.
Old socks throw a party, mismatched and bold,
While the clock on the wall shares secrets untold!

Dust motes dance like they own the place,
While the fridge hums a culinary case.
Time reschedules with a joyful clap,
In forgotten corners, there's always a map!

So let's wake the echoes, share a good laugh,
As we gather the memories, stitch a new path.
The corners may be old, but oh, what a spark,
In the timeless embrace of delightful dark!

A Journey Begins with Ray's Touch

Morning creeps with a tickling sun,
Chasing shadows, oh what fun!
Slippers dance on the wooden floor,
As dreams bid a cheeky adieu once more.

Coffee brews like bubbling laughter,
Toast pops up, a joyful crafter.
Spills and thrills, what a sight,
As morning banter takes to flight.

A cat leaps high, a dog gives chase,
Muffins roll with a giggly grace.
Each moment wraps in a cheerful jest,
A silly start, we feel so blessed.

With rays that tickle and tease our glee,
Adventure calls, "Come dance with me!"
Together we'll wander where laughter abounds,
In the glow of dawn, where joy resounds.

Dawn's Gentle Hand on Slumbering Souls

Whispers of light, a soft little poke,
As snores fill the air like a cheeky joke.
Blankets toss, and pillows fly,
Dreams stumble out with a sleepy sigh.

Cats curl tight, refusing the call,
While coffee wrestles with the morning squall.
Slippers stumble on toys left behind,
A symphony of chaos, oh so unrefined!

Waking up feels like a funny show,
As cereal spills in a lopsided flow.
A wiggle, a giggle, as socks don't align,
Morning mischief, like clockwork, divine.

Each yawning stretch, a clumsy ballet,
As the day breaks in a quirky display.
So here we are, all tangled and bright,
With the gentle hand of dawn, what a sight!

Larks Singing the Day Alive

Larks in the trees, with a chirpy spree,
Calling all cats to engage with glee.
Barking back, the dog takes a bow,
As the world awakes in a feathered row.

Breakfast becomes a melodious show,
With pancakes flipping in a joyful flow.
Syrup drizzles like laughter on plates,
Creating a breakfast that celebrates.

Sunbeam trickles through the window pane,
As kids and pets join the morning's refrain.
Chasing shadows, they romp and prance,
As the larks sing on, in their sunny dance.

Beneath this symphony, smiles abound,
With laughter echoing all around.
So let's welcome the day, no matter the strife,
In the morning chorus, we find the spirit of life.

Unwritten Pages in Morning's Book

The day unfolds, a blank page awaits,
With scribbles and doodles that fate creates.
A splash of syrup, a cat that glides,
As laughter bursts where joy abides.

Peeking out, the sun gives a grin,
Awakening giggles from deep within.
Each tick of the clock, a whimsy fair,
As dreams take flight on the morning air.

A tickly breeze engages our hair,
As breakfast burns with a tender flair.
With silly moods and coffee spills,
The morning stretches, with endless thrills.

So join me in scribbling these lines,
In unwritten tales where laughter shines.
For each dawn brings chances, oh what a look,
As we scribe our stories in morning's book.

Gentle Beginnings in the Soft Light

Morning giggles, sleepy sighs,
Grumpy cats with half-closed eyes.
The toast pops up, it's burnt again,
Coffee spills, oh what a pain!

Socks mismatched, what a sight,
Eggs are bouncing, what a flight!
A squirrel darts, a bird does squawk,
The dog just chased a wayward sock.

Children laugh, the day starts bright,
With cereal wars, oh what a fight!
Tickles and laughs, breakfast mayhem,
In the soft light, we're all in the same gym!

Joyful chaos, fun from the start,
Belly laughs that warm the heart.
Gentle beginnings, how they flow,
Life's a circus, come see the show!

Emotions Awakened by the Dawn

Birds chirp loudly, what a chorus,
They've no clue what's really in store for us.
Banging pots, and toast on the floor,
Dad slips and lands, he's not keeping score!

Mismatched slippers, the fashion faux pas,
Mom just laughs, she's our North Star.
Eggs explode, oh what a thrill,
Pancake landmines—what a skill!

Voices rising, an amusing sound,
Joy in chaos, everywhere found.
The morning dance, a clumsy show,
In the bright light, we all steal the glow!

Laughter echoes, love fills the air,
Box of cereal? Who really cares?
Emotions awaken, a fun escapade,
At dawn's soft light, our memories are made!

Tales Woven in the Early Glow

Sunlight tickles, waking a snore,
A cat has claimed the couch; the floor?
Socks on the ceiling, oh what a mess!
Who left the cereal out? Just guess!

Children giggle with glee and delight,
One steals a cookie, what a brave bite!
Mom hunts down a rogue runaway toy,
Dad finds coffee—oh joy, oh joy!

Fairy tales spun with giggles and fun,
Pirate adventures before breakfast is done.
A race to the pancakes, forks poised at hand,
In the morning glow, laughter is planned!

Mop and broom take a daily retreat,
Why clean up? We're here for a treat!
Tales woven of joy, like a fine stitch,
In the early glow, we pitch and we twitch!

The First Kiss of Solitude

Quiet moments, the world's still asleep,
Peeking out, the secrets we keep.
A worn-out robe, mismatched slippers too,
Oh the things that solitude can do!

One donut left, a sweet little prize,
Break out the coffee, let's rise and surprise!
Pajamas dance in a solo ballet,
Under the sunrise, we laugh and we play.

In the calm, a hidden delight,
The cat plots mischief in morning light.
Tea spills over, a clumsy affair,
In solitude's kiss, we've no weight to bear!

Time to sneak treats, oh what a thrill,
In this still moment, life's a good will.
A chuckle escapes in this private domain,
In the first kiss of solitude, we're never mundane!

Ghosts of Sleep in Fading Shadows

In corners dark with sleepy dust,
A sock lies there, it's lost our trust.
The cat's on guard, with stealthy paws,
Chasing dreams that have no flaws.

The lamp hums low, a ghostly buzz,
And creaks and squeaks are common fuzz.
The toaster pops, it's breakfast time,
But bread flies out, a daring climb.

A poltergeist with jam and toast,
Spreads breakfast cheer, it loves it most.
The fridge resounds with jars that chime,
In morning light, it's laughing time!

So here we wake, in sleepy cheer,
With playful spirits drawing near.
We tumble forth, our eyelids blink,
In this odd dance, we laugh and think.

A Portrait of Tranquility

A squirrel feasts on acorn snacks,
While birds debate on shiny facts.
A breeze floats in, it tips the hats,
Of flowers bright and chatty cats.

The garden gnomes hold court today,
In silent prayer, they joke and play.
The tulips nod in soft embrace,
While daisies giggle, keeping pace.

A bee flies by, it's on a quest,
To find the bloom it likes the best.
It bumps and sways, a clumsy dance,
In this grand art of bees' romance.

With every step, we weave the sound,
Of laughter shared, it spins around.
A canvas made of quirks and quirks,
In this calm space, hilarity lurks.

Morning's Breath Upon the Earth

Awake, the sun begins to rise,
With coffee steam, our sleepy eyes.
A toast gets stuck, it's quite a sight,
As jam becomes a flying kite.

The dog runs circles 'round the floor,
While socks are missing, can't ignore.
The curtains dance with playful flair,
As if they know we're unaware.

A rogue hair tie takes off to chase,
The wild bath mat in this race.
A game of tag in morning glow,
With each new dawn, it steals the show.

So as we sip our brew with cheer,
And laugh at mishaps drawing near,
This morning's breath, a funny song,
As life hums on, we all belong.

Whispers of Tomorrow's Dreams

The clock ticks soft, a sly old friend,
With secrets kept that never end.
It whispers tales of sleep-unfold,
Of wild adventures yet untold.

A pillow fight with feathery foes,
As slumber monsters strike their pose.
The bedpost creaks, a mighty ship,
Set sail for dreams on a moonlit trip.

In shadowy corners, giggles bloom,
As magic fills the sleeping room.
A fantasy, a dream-drenched play,
We wake, it's time to seize the day!

So let us dance on starlit beams,
And cherish whispers of our dreams.
With laughter threading through the seams,
Tomorrow waits, with joyful gleams.

A Canvas of Dawn's Promise

Morning spills colors on the floor,
Cats slide in, thinking it's a door.
Toast pops up with a joyful tune,
Match it with coffee, it's nearly noon.

The dog chases shadows, so spry,
While the birds gossip, oh how they fly!
Butterflies giggle, dancing in light,
As the sun wakes up, oh what a sight!

Socks left on the porch find a mate,
Rabbits debate if they're early or late.
Pancakes flip with a funny face,
In the kitchen, it's a joyful race.

With laughter echoing through the walls,
Every creak and groan, a jester calls.
Yet amidst the chaos, warmth is found,
In the canvas brightening all around.

Serenity Before the Storm

Whispers of laughter soften the air,
Dishes pile high, who even cares?
Cats curl tight in their cozy lair,
While puppies play hide and seek with despair.

Sneaky squirrels raid the backyard tree,
Gathering treasures, oh can't you see?
With every rustle, their plans unfold,
Nature's pranksters, so bold and so cold.

A pancake tower, a syrupy peak,
Unstable balance, we all take a sneak.
One little nudge sends it to fate,
And laughter erupts, never too late.

Light flickers out, now darkness looms,
But the laughter still chases the gloom.
Serenity dances before the storm,
With joy and mischief, it's never warm.

Melodies of the Rising Sun

A rooster starts the morning show,
Crowing proudly like he knows the flow.
Kettle whistles with a high-pitched song,
As sleepyheads stretch, it won't be long.

Pancakes flip like they're on a stage,
Butter melts in a syrupy rage.
Orange juice splashes in a joyful arc,
While the cat sneezes—a comedic spark!

The sun peeks in through curtains drawn,
Tickling all hearts just before the dawn.
Toys left out have their own ballet,
As giggles echo the start of play.

In this symphony of morning cheer,
Every little blunder, crystal clear.
As the day unfolds, laughter shall ring,
With the melodies of the joy we bring.

Unraveling the Night's Tapestry

Stars twinkle, sharing secrets so dear,
But morning laughs, 'Hey, I've got this sphere!
A sock on the lamp, how did it land?'
With tangled sheets, it's a chaotic band.

Bacon sizzles, a tasty ballet,
But the toast jumps out like it's in a play.
Coffee spills like a stormy brew,
While the cat yawns, "What is this view?"

Time unravels in the breakfast scene,
Where laughter and butter mix in between.
The night retreats with a playful grin,
But morning mischief is where we begin.

Unlocking joy, with every spilled cup,
The day is calling, we're ready to sup.
As we weave through the humorous plight,
Creating memories till the fall of night.

The Awakening of Forgotten Rooms

Cobwebs dance in cheeky glee,
As dust bunnies plot their spree.
The sofa squeaks a silly tune,
While curtains gossip with the moon.

A sock's lost in the laundry maze,
It's held captive for days and days.
Chairs engage in a peek-a-boo,
While a fridge emits a loud 'moo'.

The clock grins with a lazy tick,
"You can't rush fun, you silly stick!"
Light spills in with a playful wink,
As memories begin to wink.

In corners where the shadows creep,
The laughter sleeps but never weeps.
Each room a character in a play,
Where night turns into a silly day.

First Light Through Closed Windows

Sunrise tiptoes with a yawn,
Knocks on glass and then is gone.
The curtains blush, they sway and sway,
As pillows snicker at the day.

A coffee cup begins to laugh,
As spoons conspire with the half.
The toaster pops with a 'ta-da',
While crumbs scatter like a star.

The fridge hums with a gentle song,
That invites the cats to join along.
With each beam that stretches and plays,
The furniture dances in sun's rays.

Even the broom begins to jig,
As breakfast chefs perform a gig.
In this cheerful morning glow,
Each room puts on a funny show.

The Quiet Transition of Time

Tick-tock goes the sleepy clock,
Time plays tricks with every knock.
The shadows stretch, and then they bend,
While clocks pretend they don't intend.

The plates chatter on the shelf,
Wondering if they should eat themselves.
The lamps flicker with a wink,
"Is it day or night?" they think.

A calendar flips, but who would care?
Each day's a joke, a friendly dare.
As minutes slide in comfy chairs,
The seconds slip through nonchalant flares.

"Is it snack time yet?" whispers the chair,
While toys giggle without a care.
Time's a jester, playing fun,
From dusk till dawn, we all just run.

Reflections in the Morning Dew

Dewdrops cling with a twinkling grin,
Reflecting all that lies within.
A blade of grass, a tiny friend,
Winks at the sky as if to blend.

The garden gnomes share secrets bright,
About the snails and their slow flight.
Each petal blushes in the sun,
As laughter sparkles, just for fun.

Squirrels chatter in their morning raid,
While daisies dance in sunlight made.
Amidst the hues and softest sighs,
Life plays jokes under brightening skies.

In every droplet, a story dwells,
Of playful pranks and joyful spells.
As dawn breaks forth with cheerful view,
Nature giggles in the morning dew.

A Canvas of New Beginnings

At the crack of day, a rooster sings,
A bucket of paint, oh, the joy it brings.
Splatters on walls, colors gone wild,
Who needs a plan? We're all just a child.

Coffee spills dance, on the kitchen floor,
Laughter erupts, we fall, we roar.
The sun peeks in, with a smile so bright,
We paint our dreams in the morning light.

Bubbles in the bath, rubber ducks soar,
Each splash a giggle, who could ask for more?
This canvas new, with strokes that don't blend,
Chaos and joy—the best kind of trend.

Dancing with mops, making a mess,
Joyful hearts, we surely confess.
As the day unfolds, we embrace the fun,
With splashes of color, the day's just begun!

Shadows Fade into Warmth

As the sun wakes, shadows do flee,
A squirrel in pajamas, quick as can be.
Coffee brewed dark, with a sprinkle of cheer,
Even the cat gives a chuckle, I fear.

Chasing the light, the dust bunnies hop,
They twirl 'round the room like they're taking a drop.
The curtains do dance, with a breeze that's a tease,
Whispers of laughter, the chill in the freeze.

Sunlight pours in, spills on the floor,
Pancakes stack high, we're ready for more.
Butter melts slowly, syrup drips dance,
Who knew a breakfast could spark such romance?

The day shakes off night's sleepy twinge,
Joy fills the air like a surprising binge.
With laughter as light as the dappled glow,
The shadows retreat, as silliness flows.

Homeward Bound at First Light

As dawn creeps in, the birds start to sing,
I trip on my slippers, oh, what a thing!
Toast pops up, startled and hot,
I juggle my breakfast, right on the spot.

Neighbors peek out, their hair like a nest,
"What's that ruckus?" asks one, with zest.
I wave like a ninja, they surely must laugh,
As I tumble and stumble, my own comedy half.

The mailbox is bulging, letters galore,
I wonder if any are more than a chore.
The postman grins wide, a joke on his lips,
"Your day's just begun, with the morning's first sips."

With bags full of goodies, I head for the door,
Excited adventures await, I adore.
First light brings laughter, unplanned but precise,
Each step an adventure, as sweet as spice.

Gathering Threads of Daylight

Sunbeams gather, like threads of gold,
Each ray a story, waiting to be told.
We weave our moments, with laughter and cheer,
A tapestry bright, where the heart feels near.

As shadows retreat, we spin around,
Each giggle a stitch, in joy we are bound.
The loom of the day, with colors so bright,
Guides us to laughter, from morning to night.

Cuppa in hand, with a breakfast delight,
Spilled cereal dances, oh, what a sight!
The dog joins the fun, with a woof and a spin,
He leaps for the crumbs, where do I begin?

Now gathered together, we cheerfully play,
Each moment a thread, in the light of the day.
With smiles and jokes, we create our own way,
In this colorful fabric, we joyfully stay.

Dreams Fade with the Sun

In sleepy realms where dreams once spry,
A rooster crowed and gave a cry.
Pajamas worn as a fashion trend,
I chase my dreams but they won't bend.

Socks mismatched, a morning spree,
Coffee spills on my last decree.
The sun peeks in, it's time to rise,
Yet I still dream of sleepy pies.

A cat meows like a morning bell,
As I stumble like an unspun shell.
With breakfast burnt, I wave goodbye,
To dreams that fade as the sun climbs high.

Between Nightfall and Sunrise

The stars confide in whispers fair,
While I trip over my own lazy hair.
Between the dusk and dawn's sweet fight,
I ponder donuts and coffee light.

A ghostly presence—a toast I burn,
A dance with shadows—oh, what a turn!
Sneaking snacks in the darkened night,
Munching crumbs like a raccoon in flight.

As night bids farewell with a big grin,
I swear I'll get some rest—next again!
But morning laughs with a blaring light,
And I'm still tangled in dreams of delight.

Sunbeams on Forgotten Doorsteps

Dust bunnies gather like old friends,
Sunbeams tickle where laughter bends.
Forgotten doorsteps, a place to trudge,
Where sneakers squeak and old folks grudge.

A sliding door with a well-placed squeak,
Entices squirrels to chatter and sneak.
The garden gnomes with silly hats,
Join in the chuckle with curious cats.

Scoops of ice cream melt in the sun,
As kids race by, all thoughts of fun.
Old benches creak with every sway,
In sunshine's glow, what else can I say?

Embracing the Early Glow

The early glow, like pancakes stacked,
Brings out my talents, slightly whacked.
With mismatched socks and a quirky hat,
I waltz toward the fridge where leftovers chat.

Birds chirp like they've got a plan,
While I struggle to locate my can.
Ode to the butter, a slick little friend,
As toast pops up—on that I depend!

The sun's first touch, a warm embrace,
Turns morning clumsiness into grace.
With laughter ringing like chime bells' tone,
I welcome each mishap in my little zone.

A Quiet Invitation

In shadows where the whispers play,
A knock, a creak, it's time to stay.
The cat on the rug cracks a sneaky grin,
Inviting us in with a purr and a spin.

The coffee pot sings a silly tune,
As buttered toast dances to the moon.
A chair that's squeaky, a floor that squeals,
This cozy abode has its funny feels.

The clock on the wall has an offbeat chime,
It echoes our laughter, a rhythm in rhyme.
Each corner a story, a giggle, a light,
In this jumbled haven, everything's right.

With socks in the fridge and shoes on the rack,
Our gathering blooms like a quirky snack.
So grab a corncob, let the laughter flow,
This quiet invitation, we're ready to grow.

Glistening Dreams Unfurled

Dreams glisten brightly on a dish,
Like bubbles that twirl in a fruity swish.
The sponge cake wiggles, it jumps, and it jives,
While cookies do cartwheels, oh how they thrive!

The fridge's a kingdom of melted delight,
With jam jars that waltz in the soft, dim light.
A butter parade, cheerful and bright,
Unfolding each morning with whimsical bites.

The pancake flips higher than anyone thinks,
Landing in syrup, it sparkles and winks.
With each joyous puff, our dreams take flight,
In the kitchen's embrace, everything feels right.

So raise up a toast with a glass full of glee,
To glistening hopes and a wild jubilee.
Together we gather, let merriment reign,
In the dance of our dreams, we'll never complain.

The Promise of Tomorrow

The sun peeks in through curtains of lace,
A mischievous grin on its bright, golden face.
With slippers all tangled and hair full of dreams,
We dive into breakfast, exploding with beams.

The toast suddenly jumps, a warm, crispy cheer,
As the peanut butter whispers, "I'm spreading good cheer!"
With each silly spill, the giggles take flight,
In this silly jaunt, the future feels bright.

A cat on the ledge gives a knowing meow,
While cereal swims, it's a raucous row.
The promise of later dances in air,
With mischief and planning, we boldly prepare.

As coffee cups clink in a bubbly delight,
Our hearts full of laughter, everything's right.
We look to tomorrow with glee and with doubt,
For life is a riddle, a joyful shout.

Softly Spoken Dawn

A gentle nudge from the world outside,
The sleepy sun whispers, 'Come join the ride!'
With sleepy faces and yawns that could shake,
We stumble together, a wobbly wake.

The kettle's a drummer, its steam swirling high,
While toast does the tango as we pass it by.
Mismatched socks giggle from the basket below,
In the early embrace where our stories will grow.

The flower vase hums a tune all its own,
With daisies gossiping of everything grown.
Each corner a chuckle, sweet whispers of grace,
In this softly spoken dawn, we find our place.

So gather the warmth from the sunshine's first glow,
With laughter and pastries, let the good times flow.
In this cozy moment, so charmingly drawn,
We revel together, from dusk until dawn.

Whispers of Morning Light

The rooster crows, but I just grin,
Dreams of bacon dance within.
Sunshine peeks through the curtain fold,
Tickles my nose, brave and bold.

Coffee brews with a playful glee,
Cat steals a sip, and oh, the spree!
Socks mismatched on my feet,
Morning madness can't be beat.

Toast pops up, it couldn't wait,
Jumps up high like it's on a date.
Butterfly kisses a little jam,
Breakfast chaos, such a slam!

With each giggle, the day unfolds,
A lively tale, that never gets old.
We dance beneath the gleaming sky,
In this morning fun, we fly!

Awakening Shadows

The shadows yawn, stretching wide,
A squirrel scampers, it can't hide.
Branches sway, a leafy cheer,
Nature's antics, loud and clear.

Waking up to pancake flights,
Flour flying in morning sights.
Bubbles bounce from the sink,
Even dishes start to wink!

The dog chases after a bee,
A surprising twist, oh what a spree!
Morning banter fills the air,
With giggling friends, nothing is rare.

Finally, we tumble outside,
Joy and laughter, a wild ride.
Waving goodbyes to sleepy night,
Awakening shadows in morning light!

Echoes of a New Day

Echoes ring in a sleepy town,
Lamp posts wear a sleepy frown.
Birds compete in a morning race,
Singing out in a feathered embrace.

Joggers trip over their own feet,
Their laughter makes the morning sweet.
A duck parade through the grassy way,
Quacking jokes to start the day.

Neighbors scurry, tripping on shoes,
Chasing the sun, spreading the news.
With coffee cups clinking in the fun,
It feels like a mad dash to the sun!

Chasing laughter in the morning air,
Echoes of joy, everywhere.
Life dances on a vibrant stage,
A new day, a brand new page!

Solace in Sunrise

In sunlight's glow, the cats conspire,
Plotting naps on a window wire.
The world awakes in a lazy huff,
Snoring still, oh, it's rough!

Pancakes flip, and they stick!
They jump around, a breakfast trick.
The squirrel's laughter fills the air,
Chasing crumbs without a care.

The clock ticks slow, the toaster beeps,
Time for giggles, not for sleeps.
Bubbles float from the dish as well,
A bubbly morning, can't you tell?

In this dawn, we find our cheer,
Laughter dances, hold it dear.
Solace found in a playful beam,
A new day started with a dream!

A Tapestry Woven in Gold

In a morning so bright, the cat starts to yawn,
While socks dance around, as if they have sworn.
The toast jumps with joy, like it's aiming for flight,
And jam makes a splash, much to everyone's delight.

A hat on the dog, which looks rather grand,
He struts with a swagger, like he's in a band.
The coffee pot whistles, with a tune quite absurd,
As birds chirp their gossip, a comical herd.

Pancakes stack high, but they wobble and sway,
They think they're the stars of this breakfast ballet.
The teaspoon is laughing, it's juggling with cheer,
As syrup starts slipping, oh dear, oh dear!

In this home of mischief, the laughter won't cease,
Even the fridge joins in, with a rattle of peace.
Each morning's a circus, full of giggles and gold,
In a tapestry woven, with stories untold.

Sunlit Paths and Hidden Stories

The sun peeks through curtains, with a playful grin,
Coffee stains laughter, as the day begins.
The dog's got a shoe, it's a game of huge stakes,
And off goes the squirrel, in a dance that it makes.

The pancakes are flipping, one lands on the floor,
And a rogue little spoon starts a raucous uproar.
The cat's on a mission, to scale to the ledge,
While dad reads the news, but he's lost on the hedge.

A broom takes a leap, like it's straight out of dreams,
Chasing crumbs like it's wild, with its dusting regimes.
The curtains are swaying, with a secretive sway,
Whispering tales of the antics at play.

In sunlight drenched laughter, the moments collide,
Each day tells a story, with joy as our guide.
Paths winding with echoes of giggles and glee,
And oh how we cherish such folly, you see!

Flickers of Life Amidst the Fog

In the fog of the morn, there's a twitching of leaves,
The kettle's on fire, a dance that it weaves.
The toast, it protests, 'I'm not burnt, just inspired!'
While butter rejoices, 'Now my chance has arrived!'

The fog lifts a corner, revealing a cat,
Who's plotting a scheme, to outsmart a rat.
And coffee's debating, with tea on the side,
Which one's the champion, with caffeine for pride.

A sock flies from nowhere, convincing a mate,
'Let's escape these confines, it's time to abate!'
The chairs are conspiring, a new dance they've found,
While breakfast keeps laughing, it's a festival sound.

With smiles that are glimmering, and jokes in the fog,
Each morning delivers a tale, just like a cog.
Flickers of life, in confusion we find,
The funny in mornings, forever entwined.

Morning Rituals in a Silent World

The dawn's hush is broken by a clatter and bang,
As breakfast begins with a bright rap and clang.
The cereal leaps, with its crunchy delight,
And the spoon starts to dance, as if it's in flight.

A cat on the counter, quite proud of its stand,
Surveys the whole kingdom — what a sight so grand!
The plants seem to chuckle, in their green little way,
As the toaster sizzles, 'Just give me one day!'

Omelets flip high, in a jubilant spin,
While dad spills the milk, with a cheeky little grin.
The dog shakes his head, as if to agree,
That mornings, though hectic, bring humor to tea.

In this silent old world, laughter holds sway,
Each ritual adding a slapstick bouquet.
With giggles at breakfast, the day starts anew,
And mornings are filled with mischief and hue.

Reflections on the Threshold

A door creaks wide, the morning sighs,
A cat chased a ghost, oh how it flies!
Coffee's brewing, sings an old tune,
While socks dance around like they're at a moon.

The mirror's cracked, my hair's a fight,
I think I've lost my comb last night.
A roach plays tag with my old shoe,
I think I'll let them share the view!

Sun peeks in, and shadows yawn,
A breakfast feast of burnt-out bacon spawn.
The fridge hums softly, in a good mood,
While yesterday's pizza gets a rude brood.

At last, I step, the world's a whirl,
A neighbor's kid spins, watch him twirl!
Each step is laughter, a jig of delight,
Who knew mornings could be such a sight?

Dawn's Embrace

In the kitchen, pots and pans collide,
I'm up for adventure, let's take a ride!
The toast jumps up, it's lost its place,
While my slippers chase in a silly race.

Sunlight beams through the window's frame,
I swear that dog just called my name!
Milk's on the counter, a puddle of white,
It shouted the news, "I'm a cereal blight!"

The cat's on the table, surveying its throne,
While I just wonder when I'll be grown.
A sock on my head, I dance like a clown,
With laughter ringing, I twirl all around.

At the end of the day, I sit with a grin,
What a funny start, let the chaos begin!
Dawn's bright embrace, a comedy show,
Who knew waking up could be such a glow?

Beneath the Glistening Veil

Under covers, dreams run wild,
A dancing bear? Yes, I'm that child!
The curtain flutters, a breeze so sweet,
While slippers do a jig with my two left feet.

A pancake flips, but misses the plate,
It lands on the floor, oh what a fate!
With syrup streams making their way,
The floor's now a treat, come what may!

Laughter echoes through the daylight air,
As I spot a bug with a flair for hair.
It's waltzing on counters, a tiny ballet,
What a start to another bright day!

With toast on my nose, I embrace the fun,
Every new moment is a race to run!
Under the veil of a day yet untold,
Life's quirkiest moments were meant to unfold.

In the Glow of Breaking Day

In shades of peach, my cereal waits,
With a side of giggles and plateful of fates.
A squirrel outside scurries and dives,
Bounding past windows, it surely thrives.

The kettle whistles, it sounds like a tune,
While I juggle cups under the watchful moon.
A toast to the mess and the chaos it brings,
For laughter's our anthem, oh the joy that it sings!

The cat's now lounging, a prince in repose,
I chuckle at life's little comedy shows.
Pajamas and dreams, still wrapped in delight,
In the glow of breaking, we dance through the light.

With every new dawn, we tumble and roll,
A rollercoaster ride, that's the goal!
In each twist of morning, a giggling sway,
We find fun and laughter in every way.

Light Disturbing the Stillness

In the early hours, a rooster sings,
Awakening dreams and odd little things.
A cat on the windowsill chases a bug,
While a coffee pot gurgles, it's feeling snug.

The curtains dance with a cheerful sway,
As a sock on the floor begs for some play.
The milk spills out as the dog runs by,
In this circus of mornings, oh my, oh my!

The toast pops up in a little surprise,
A burnt offering to the hungry skies.
With dance moves like Elvis, the bread sings loud,
While the clock just giggles, feeling quite proud.

Yet, amid the chaos, a laugh takes flight,
The sponge hums a tune, it's a marvelous sight.
With morning light tickling everything near,
Tomorrow's antics, we have naught a fear.

Vignettes of Dawn's Rebirth

Sunrise spills syrup on petals so bright,
The bees start their buzzing, claiming their right.
A squirrel drops acorns with clumsy finesse,
As the trees dodge raindrops in humorous dress.

Birds wear their best suits, they chirp and they chirp,
As they plan their revenge on the old sleeping sirp.
The mailbox yawns wide, it's bored of its role,
While the postman delivers—his dance is quite whole.

A pancake flops down, wanting a friend,
As laughter erupts; the maple trees bend.
A bike tire squeaks like a silly old man,
As morning unfolds in a whimsical plan.

So here's to the dawn, with its quirks and its glee,
Each dawn brings mishaps like leaves from a tree.
In these vignettes, we find joy in the mess,
Embracing the chaos, we lightheartedly bless.

Beneath the Veil of First Light

With the first glimmers, the curtains collide,
As the dog finds the couch in a search for a ride.
The blender's a monster, it roars with delight,
While pancakes do somersaults, flipping outright.

The fridge yawns open, a spectacle grand,
Where leftovers argue, 'who's taking the stand?'
A spoon breaks the silence, a fork joins the fray,
In the early light's dance, there's laughter at play.

The slippers hop around, playing tag with the floor,
While the cat philosophizes, 'what's life really for?'
The coffee beans chuckle as they take a dive,
In a miracle morning, so slumberingly alive.

So let's raise a toast to the silly and spry,
In the sheen of first light, we'll giggle and sly.
For beneath every dawn, there's a jest waiting sly,
A comical gift with every blink of an eye.

Where Memories Embrace the Present

Time wears its pajamas, clashing in hues,
As laughter ignites like a thrilling muse.
The past rolls its eyes at the present's wild antics,
In a whirlwind of moments, each day enchants us.

A skateboard rolls by, with a wink and a twist,
While yesterday's failures, like ghosts, can't resist.
Socks lost in the laundry start plotting their plan,
For a daring escape into dreams of a fan.

The coffee pot winks, summoning spirits,
The memories giggle, oh, how they hear it!
Each smile, a treasure, cementing the day,
As the present embraces what pasts can't convey.

So let's gather our stories, weave them with glee,
A tapestry of laughter, for all to see.
In this delightful embrace of moments so bright,
We find joy intertwined in the fabric of light.

When the World Awakens

Sunbeams dance on sleepy heads,
Cats chase shadows, dodging beds.
Coffee spills in morning cheer,
While toast takes a leap, oh dear!

Birds sing songs that make us grin,
As the dog plans his grand spin.
The clock ticks loud, a funny beast,
For breakfast, we all need a feast.

With yawns that echo, we all rise,
Finding socks and telling lies.
The fridge hums a merry tune,
While we debate, 'Is it too soon?'

The world awakes, a quirky play,
With giggles that just lead the way.
Mismatched shoes and rumpled hair,
Welcome to mornings full of flair!

Morning's Gentle Tapestry

Mist swirls in like a sneaky cat,
Chasing leaves, where did they sat?
Pancakes flip like acrobats,
Full of syrup, what's the stats?

The kettle whistles, sounds so grand,
A perfect brew made by hand.
Squirrels plot their clever heist,
The birdseed's gone; oh, how nice!

With every flap and jump they make,
The morning's softly bound to shake.
Cereal spills, a crunchy mess,
"Who ate the last?," we must confess.

Laughter erupts, spills on the floor,
As we dance to the breakfast score.
Waking dreams in sunlight's glow,
A tapestry of morning's show!

A Symphony of New Horizons

Dawn's orchestra begins to play,
With every note, the world's ballet.
The rooster crows, a loud surprise,
While sleepy heads rub their eyes.

Pajamas stretch in comfy grace,
As we argue whose turn to race.
The milk's gone sour, how absurd!
While cats plot how to steal a bird.

Joggers leap on sidewalks wide,
While coffee-drinkers smile with pride.
Birds belt tunes with perfect flair,
A symphony fills the fresh air.

As the sun climbs high, we cheer,
"A brand new day is finally here!"
With smiles wide and hearts in tune,
We welcome the day, oh how soon!

Rays of Possibility

Light spills in through the windowpane,
Proving the sun is not to blame.
Shoes untied, a funny sight,
As we stumble to delight.

The toast pops, a dance of heat,
Fork in hand, a morning treat.
With breakfast joys upon our face,
We brave the day with silly grace.

The mailman trips while on his route,
While grumpy geese begin to shout.
Neighbors laugh, it starts to spread,
Morning giggles, enough said!

With rays of hope and silly dreams,
We navigate life's funny schemes.
So here's to dawn, bright and free,
A chance to laugh, just you and me!

www.ingramcontent.com/pod-product-compliance
Lightning Source LLC
Chambersburg PA
CBHW060137230426
43661CB00003B/465